Woman Sitting at the Machine, Thinking

Poems 1978 - 1987

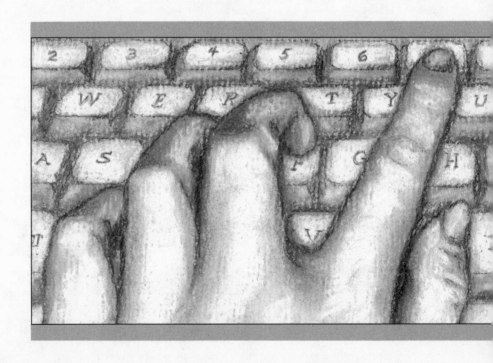

Preface by

Red Letter Press, Seattle, Washington

Woman Sitting at the Machine, Thinking

Poems by Karen Brodine

Meridel Le Sueur ■ Introduction by Merle Woo

© 1990 by Red Letter Press
5018 Rainier Avenue South
Seattle, Washington 98118 ● 206-722-2453
All rights reserved
Printed in the United States of America

Library of Congress Cataloging in Publication Data
Brodine, Karen.
Woman sitting at the machine, thinking.
I. Title.
PS3552.R622W66   1990   811'.54   87-83121
ISBN 0-932323-01-4

First Edition

Some of these poems first appeared in *An Ear to the
Ground: An Anthology of Contemporary
American Poetry, Backbone, Common Lives/Lesbian Lives,
Contact II, Crab Creek Review, Ergo!,
Feminist Poetics, Fireweed: A Feminist Quarterly,
The Freedom Socialist, Greenfield Review,
Hanging Loose, Home Planet News, Hurricane Alice, Ikon,
Lesbian Poetry, New Lesbian Writing, Out and About,
Poets On, The Portland Alliance, Practicing Angels:
A Contemporary Anthology of San Francisco Bay Area
Poetry, Room, Sinister Wisdom, Soup, Synapse, Transfer,*
and *When I Am An Old Woman I Shall Wear Purple.*

The title poem was published in 1984 in a limited edition
chapbook by Radical Women Publications, Seattle,
Washington. Sections of the title poem were also included
in a theatre production, "Work Poems in Performance:
Coffee Break Secrets," created and performed by Word of
Mouth Productions, Jamaica Plain, Massachusetts.

Videotaped readings by Karen Brodine of some poems in
this collection are available from the American Poetry
Archives at the Poetry Center, San Francisco State
University, 1600 Holloway, San Francisco, California 94132.

Contents

Photographs

My thanks to David Joseph, Merle Woo,
Carol Tarlen, Rozwell Spafford, Gail Wiley,
Helen Gilbert and the Freedom Socialist Party
for their help in publishing this book.

Karen Brodine
San Francisco, California
July 1987

Preface

I AM GLAD I lived this long with all its pain to see and hear the new women like karen brodine appearing out of the wound—the endangered womb rising from the patriarchal terrors of the city—as woman as worker as revolutionary with new consciousness and expression. . .in my life as an exploited woman I could see only in pieces in ruins and pain and I sing hosannas for this woman and this work. . .she is not alone not a single woman but with the visibility of a woman rising into freedom of struggle and enflaming—engendering the flame of power of the word out of the bonds of the exploiter, the oppressor. . .under the heel of the conqueror she rises in rich clear cadences like a great unfolding plant of nature from the nature of woman.

Reading poetry with her in san francisco years ago I felt her strength and simplicity and purefire bursting out of her experiences at the forge of exploitation. . .a clear sound of the hammer on the anvil. . .her poetry becomes a political anvil—sparks fly—fire is sparked from the vigor and the passion.

As a poet wounded in my time. . .driven down into the pits . . .I took her hand. . .for it is hard to forge poetry words like this from the years of pain of her mothers of our mothers. . .to make a form beautiful and visible that speaks in the woman wound that ignites the fire of change. . .illuminates the dark and speaks for us.

The womans movement moves in the meaning of these poems and her vivid making visible of woman class and revolution. . .we must embody these *whole* to conceive of ourselves and our liberation.

These poems are a flame ignited by struggle and the strong and communal spirit of a woman poet in the full and rich sense of that naming. . .in these poems she has made a whole struggle from the woman struggle the class struggle the image of change the perpetual growth of revolution the igniting of revolution. . .I need this as I need food.

Meridel Le Sueur
Hudson, Wisconsin
September 1987

Introduction

A POET'S POET and a people's poet—that was Karen Brodine.

And in this, her fourth, her most mature, and her best book of poetry, she powerfully expressed her great love of language. Language to her was fivefold: basic, clear communication, our primary connection to others; imagery and symbol; a conveyor of emotion; a medium and exhortation to change; and a means of telling us about herself and how she felt about the world.

Brodine's profound respect for the word impelled her to take the care to find the truest and most appropriate expression of what she experienced. She unerringly found the most fitting form, the most arresting patterns and rhythms for her words. And this great skill derived from her intense concern with *content*. Content determines form, of course, and here the reader will find many rich forms, for Brodine had a great variety of new and unique things to tell us, many confidences emerging from her private and political growth.

An Old Victorian once said that beauty is only fineness of expression. Art for art's sake, in other words. But when an artist blends this capacity for creating perceptible beauty with a life of energetic and full engagement, then the audience gets so very much more than surface esthetics. In Brodine one finds beauty and love, the strong sense of living among and with people, the delicacy and funk of grit, struggle, flesh, bone and heart. If you want "art," you'll be satisfied. But if you are looking for more, for meaning and poetry, for some essences about modern life, for some clear-eyed solutions and good reasons for hope, you'll get that, too.

Brodine is not one of those poets who play with language; for her, language in and of itself was not its own *raison d'être*. Nor was she an outsider, a dispassionate observer of the world from the stance of the lofty *artiste*. Poet Brodine was a working woman and a political activist, and these aspects of her persona bring an immediate relevance to the quality of her writing. People are primary: the common individual in American society and the global human condition are of central import to her. In a particularly real, specific and imaginative sense, she saw and depicted women, people of color, lesbians and gays, workers, family, and friends just as we are—but she saw us with uncommon respect, humor, confidence and affinity. And we find ourselves believing that we, the people, are indeed courageous and are the actual pivots of social change.

Brodine's shining belief in us inspires a will to effect a cataclysmic change from capitalist dehumanization and cruel exploitation to a socialist community of equals with total opportunity to achieve our fullest potential.

This book reveals Karen Brodine, and through her are revealed our own lives on the job, as we labor, socialize with, and organize with our co-workers. Through these poems, we'll be ignited by the joy and inspiration of issues-activism, of mass demonstrations and picket lines. And we'll hear the daily buzz of commotion and camaraderie inside the Freedom Socialist Party, where political feminism sings out its revolutionary songs.

Brodine's life and Brodine's poetry are about the *interaction* of people and institutions, and the crucial connections among mind, body, spirit, society and nature. A philosophical materialist opposed to egocentric idealism, she recognized, adjusted to, and used in her writing all that is real: her lesbian sexuality, her dreams, the symbols and images that occurred to her, her conscious intellectual life, the gamut of her emotions and ideas. Her writing is a silver fishnet—you pull up one strand and the rest of her world comes up along with it. This poet was together, congruent, rooted in terra firma as she soared into the spheres.

This extraordinary, slim little book teaches us volumes about the potentials of language and humanity. It is a human symphony with themes and movements.

Woman Sitting at the Machine, Thinking, the first section, is about a typesetter who not only reproduces information, but also *thinks while she works.* She does her work well, hates her boss, sympathizes with her colleagues—and daydreams.

Fireweed, section two, is a loose-leaf poem, featuring leaves of multiple colors, angles, and sizes. It is loose and easy, depicting memories and illuminations.

The title poem of section three, *Here, Take My Words,* deals with Brodine's grandmother, isolated in a convalescent home, exemplifying the sad plight of the old and sick in an old and sick society. The poem is also about language again, with truth told through the medium of an apparently illogical and crazy old woman. The usual amenities of socialization do not matter in the wards, time is suspended, and symbols abound.

This section on mother and grandmother, their lives and deaths, their political involvement and their teaching, conveys vividly, and often with affectionate humor, the family tenacity and dedication to principle that were so paramount in the direction of Brodine's life.

Here and in the final section, *Left Feather,* runs a recurring theme of censorship—the silencing of her grandmother through a series of job discharges during the McCarthy days, the silencing of women in the home and in society; the pervasive intimidation and repression of all oppressed people, then and now; the outlawing of touch and speech and radicalism. But always, always, Brodine presents the opposite pole as well, where irrepressible rebels speak out, protest, work collectively in self-defense, and organize for advancement.

Another recurring theme in the final section is Brodine's startlingly candid approach to her cancer. There is no self-pity here. But the disease is ever-present, a painful and bitter reminder of her own mortality, and we become the beneficiaries of her vision of what life is and could be, and her heroic assertion and demonstration of the courage and combativeness one can summon in the face of death.

Brodine has also given us a profound appreciation for little details we take for granted: rain, wind, trees, lakes, and our own nutty quirkiness, absolute loveliness, lovability, and sensuality.

Her own words, from "Letter to Meridel Le Sueur," best express the relations between language and life and commitment that guided her sense and sensibility:

Everyday the determination to grow stronger. . . .

The other night I saw hundreds of minute horses, red sea horses, bobbing in the ocean, all our words, our lives streaming up from the deep—raw, skinned, nerves exposed, but swimming and bobbing, red apples, banners, clay, blood, the color to revive this planet. And Meridel, if your words swim up and are sustained and move us, then I know my words can do that too.

Meridel, Hien Luong, Clara Fraser, Nellie Wong, so many women shouting out we belong to the whole red-stained, cloud-rimmed earth and brimming oceans and the light belongs to us all, knowing the earth must be turned, baring the rich dark soil, knowing that we must take power all together in the long run

for we are the left feathers of the left wing fierce dappled sleek span the whole body depends upon

Merle Woo
San Francisco, California
January 1988

Woman Sitting at the Machine, Thinking

A series of work poems

she thinks about everything at once without making a mistake.
no one has figured out how to keep her from doing this thinking
while her hands and nerves also perform every delicate complex
function of the work. this is not automatic or deadening.
try it sometime. make your hands move quickly on the keys
fast as you can, while you are thinking about:

the layers, fossils. the idea that this machine she controls
is simply layers of human workhours frozen in steel, tangled
in tiny circuits, blinking out through lights like hot, red eyes.
the noise of the machine they all sometimes wig out to, giddy,
zinging through the shut-in space, blithering atoms;
everyone's hands paused mid-air above the keys
while Neil or Barbara solo, wrists telling every little thing,
feet blipping along, shoulders raggly.

she had always thought of money as solid, stopped.
but seeing it as moving labor, human hours, why that means
it comes back down to her hands on the keys, shoulder aching,
brain pushing words through fingers through keys, trooping
out crisp black ants on the galleys. work compressed into
instruments, slim computers, thin as mirrors, how could
numbers multiply or disappear, squeezed in sideways like that
but they could, they did, obedient and elegant, how amazing.
the woman whips out a compact, computes the cost,
her face shining back from the silver case
her fingers, sharp tacks, calling up the digits.

when she sits at the machine, rays from the cathode stream
directly into her chest. when she worked as a clerk, the rays
from the xerox angled upward, striking her under the chin.
when she waited tables the micro oven sat at stomach level.
when she typeset for Safeway, dipping her hands in processor
chemicals, her hands burned and peeled and her chest ached
from the fumes.

well we know who makes everything we use or can't use.
as the world piles itself up on the bones of the years,
so our labor gathers.

while we sell ourselves in fractions. they don't want us all
at once, but hour by hour, piece by piece. our hands mainly
and our backs. and chunks of our brains. and veiled expressions
on our faces, they buy. though they can't know what actual
thoughts stand behind our eyes.

then they toss the body out on the sidewalk at noon and at five.
then they spit the body out the door at sixty-five.

■

each morning:

fresh thermos of coffee at hand; for the slowing down, shift
gears, unscrew the lid of the orange thermos, pour out a whiff
of home, morning paper, early light. a tangible pleasure
against the unlively words.

funny, though. this set of codes slips through my hands, a
loose grid of shadows with big gaps my own thoughts sneak
through. . .

Call format o five. Reports, Disc 2, quad left
return. name of town, address, zip. quad left
return. rollalong and there you are.
done with this one. start the next.

call format o five. my day so silent yet taken up with words.
floating through the currents and cords of my wrists
into the screen and drifting to land, beached pollywogs.
all this language handled yet the room is so silent.
everyone absorbed in feeding words through the machines.

enter file execute.

Call file Oceana. name of town, Pacifica. name of street, Arbor.
thinking about lovemaking last night, how it's another land,
another set of sounds, the surface of the water, submerged,
then floating free, the delicate fabric of motion and touch
knit with listening and humming and soaring.
never a clear separation of power because it is both our power
at once. hers to speak deep in her body and voice to her own
rhythms. mine to ride those rhythms out and my own,
and call them out even more. a speaking together from body
to mouth to voice.

replace file Oceana.
call file Island.

Scroll up. . . . . .scroll down.
What is there to justify?

the words gliding on the screen like the seal at the aquarium,
funny whiskers, old man seal, zooming by upside down
smirking at the crowd, mocking us
and his friends the dolphins, each sharp black and cream marking
streamlined as the water

huh. ugh, they want this over and over:
M A Y 1   M A Y 1   M A Y 1   M A Y 1   M A Y 1 enough?
M A Y 1   M A Y 1

once I have typeset all the pages, I run the job out on tape
and clip it to the videosetter to be punched out.
then I swing out the door to get another job.

down the stairs into the cramped room where Mary and Rosie
and Agnes sit in the limp draft of one fan.
"must be 95 in here." "yeah, and freezing in the other room."
"got to keep the computers cool, you know."

back up the stairs past management barricaded
behind their big desks on the way to everything.
on the way to the candy machine.
on the way to the bathroom.
on the way to lunch.
I pretend they are invisible.
I pretend they have great big elephant ears.

and because they must think we are stupid in order
to push us around, *they* become stupid.
knowing "something's going on," peering like moles.
how can they know the quirk of an eyebrow behind their back?
they suspect we hate them because they know
what they are doing to us—but we are only
stupid Blacks or crazy Puerto Ricans, or dumb blonds.

we are their allergy, their bad dream.
they need us too much, with their talk of
"carrying us" on the payroll.
we carry them, loads of heavy, dull metal,
outmoded and dusty.
they try to control us, building partitions,
and taking the faces off the phones.
they talk to us slow and loud,
HOW ARE YOU TODAY? HERE'S A CHECK FOR YOU.
As if it were a gift.

we say—even if they stretched tape
across our mouths
we could still speak to one another
with our eyebrows.

■

hours staring me in the face
miles of straight copy
singlespaced, shut in.

when I called my mother
her words were all
turned but not quite is that
every perfect thing isn't sense,
I can't, she says, can't talk about it.
when I call her, the floor drops inches
and I am trying to be cheer.
wh-whts the matter? she says.

mother wears a dress all of blue
fabric of tiny wires and messages
veins knotted together, snagging,
and the hem gaping down
where the stitching ripped out.

don't care if things are hard
just want a whole cloth
not all these unravelled scraps and me
a rough thread trying to gut them
together, in and out.

when I see the boss, I hold
my face clear and solemn, thinking
pig. pig. it's true, too.
not rhetorical.

"if we stick you in the little room
with the heat on, you'll be happy.
that's what you wanted."

"you're an electronic technician,
not a typesetter. you're lucky
to be shut out of the union."

I know that typesetters
grow more capillaries
in our fingertips
from all that use.

here's a test: cut my fingers
and see if I bleed more.

■

knowledge this power owned, not shared
owned and hoarded
to white men, lock stock dollar
skill passed down from manager
to steal, wrench it back
knowledge is something we have
this is the bitters column
around the chair, toe stubbing the floor
and I am here, legs twisted
on our own time the words clarify
with all we are not taught
I will know it and use it burning
I sneak it home and copy it
the Puerto Rican janitor, the older
woman, the Black women, our heads
held over stolen not granted
in my stomach for all the access
I have to sneak
language is something
get my hands on the machine
he takes it all as his right
eating lunch for granted his whole life
get my hands on the book
he's being taught what I am not
angry words swallowing my throat

to take   to take it back

    and open   and ribbon out   and share

The Bitters Column.

2 hours till lunch.
1 hour till lunch.
43 minutes till lunch.
13 minutes till lunch.
LUNCH.

they write you up if you're three minutes late.
three write-ups and you're out.

I rush back from lunch, short-cut
through the hall to the door
locked like the face of a boss.

I tug at the door, definitely locked.
peer in through the glass, watery and dark,
see two supervisors standing 25 yards in,
talking, faces turned away.
oh good, I think, they'll let me in.
I knock on the glass, cold to my fist.
not too loud, just enough to let them know.
they glance at me, continue talking.
I knock again, louder.
one man looks right at me, turns his back.
I am furious, let me in!
and knock again, my fist white where it is
clenched. BAM BAM BAM pause
BAM BAM BAM BAM BAM
they don't even look up.
I knock harder and harder, the glass
shaking in its frame.
I imagine my hand smashing through the pane,
shaking their collars, bloody but triumphant.

Sleepy afternoon. . .halfway through typing a long page
about building specifications, lost, wandering
through strange buildings, wide deep fields at dusk,
trying to find the way home.

I reach a deserted building, a warehouse, fenced off.
people hurry to work, not stopping to talk.
a low-level murmur hovers below the surface, like the
slight draft that makes the hair on your arm lift.
birds clot on the aerials, the light out of whack.

we notice a tightness right below the hollow of the neck
gathering to a deep chestpain, slowmoving and thick.
we notice it like smog, waking up each morning
short-breathed and headachy. the officials say nothing's wrong,
any slippage is small, no measurable effects gather.

none of us talk outloud about this to anyone.

now though, crowds begin to pool, huddling together.
I hurry to a circle of women, where a girl dodges cops.
she is agile, darting back and forth, panting,
slippery as soap, her hair damp and glistening.
they lunge, she skips, twists, breaks from the circle
and runs. we race after her in a tumbling crowd,
she is at my ear, whispering, "money. . .burning. . .tell. . .
say. . .shout."

we are afraid, locked in a windowless building, guarded.
the pain is still here the way summer heat insists.
I repeat the words which are about the phony soap
the guards have handed us, sickly sweet,
"will it wash it will it wash it away" and another
woman joins me, "soap fake soap," and another
and now all of us are chanting and the ones guarding us
look uncertain, scared, as if they too wonder
and we are all chanting and shouting now,
"fake soap, will it wash it won't it wash it away."

half-empty streets, the calm of the warehouse district
oversize buildings like airplane hangars, expect to see
halfbuilt skeletons of planes or ships gliding the wide
rivers of the streets. nothing bustling here.
like early morning walks at home in the woods.
licorice plants flourish. the noises are big here,
not the tiny picky noises of downtown streets.

signs scrawl one wall, "US Out of El Salvador" next to a
shiny long car, must be the boss's Cadillac, next to that,
an old chev, the cadillac of onions, paint peeling, settling
into its flat tire, looks tired, looks permanent.

ha, remember that dream now, Rose and me in a great circle
of people straggling over scraped bare dirt, no green plants
and we're walking, and I realize this is a musicians' union
and we are singing the Internationale in jazz rhythm.
"let each stand in their place, we shall be all."
the buildings around us are plastered with hundreds of
red stickers that shout STRIKE STRIKE STRIKE
a woman begins to sing of all the people that work here
and the song is a list of their names and their deeds.

■

Line corrections
Interview with Leola S.
Typesetter: Karen B.

Born in Shreveport, Leola
independence is important, she
one of fourteen children, her
housecleaning in San Mateo
divorced now, she lives alone in
serving dinner from 4-5 pm every
starting pay 1.53 per
hour

she and some co-workers
today more than ever in U.S.
history

posed to discrimination by sex,
race, color, religious or national
origin

more women go to work in

enter the labor
70 percent of the average wage
Black women lowest paid of
to organize the continuing fight
determined to be heard
plaints against unfair policies
something worth fighting for
sector of the working class
women

Rivera's mural, the women, rows of them
similar, yet each unique, their hands
the focus of the art
bodies solid, leaning forward, these women,
facing the voices, knowledge running through them

language the most basic of industry
to gather our food
to record exchange
to give warning and call for help
to praise courage
it flows through our hands and into metal
they think it doesn't touch us

a typesetter changes man to person
will they catch her?
She files one job under union,
another under lagoon,
another under cash

what if you could send anything in and call it out again?
I file jobs under words I like—red, buzz, fury
search for tiger, execute
the words stream up the screen till tiger trips the halt
search for seal   search for strike
search for the names of women

we could circle our words around the world
like dolphins streaking through water their radar
if the screens were really in the hands of experts: us.
think of it—our ideas whipping through the air
everything stored in an eyeflash
our whole history, ready and waiting.

at night switching off the machines one by one
each degree of quiet a growing pleasure
we swallow the silence after hours of steady noise
the last machine harrumphs off and it is so visibly quiet
switch off the fluorescent lights and it is so quietly dark

I say, goodby, see you tomorrow, and relax down the stairs
into the cavernous shop where the paper is stored
near the presses, huge cardboard cylinders of newsprint
stacked up ceiling high.

I curve toward the door in the shadows
smells sweet like a big barn
calm snowbanks these spools, or tree trunks
in the light sifting through the glazed windows

walking tired through the resting plant
past huge breathing rolls of paper
waiting to be used

some buildings never sleep
round the clock
three eight hour shifts
seven days a week
centrifugal force irons us flat
to the blank walls, speeding,
whirling, intent as astronauts,
eyes toward the clock,
hands on the keys,
shoulders pressed against the chair.

some buildings never sleep
never shut down
roaring and roaring and we shout,
WHAT DID YOU SAY? HUH? WHAT?
WHERE IS THE? WHAT DID YOU SAY?

continuous paper streams from the room
words ratatat through our brains
trains and earthquakes shudder the walls
the long whistle of wind under the door
all we know of outside

remember that fish
that lives so deep
it has grown its own light
energy glaring out the bulbs
of its eyes
remember that fish formed flat
under fathoms of water
bones streamlined as ribs of steel
precise and efficient, formed in duress,
reaching, spinning the tough wire
of its own life, and long before Edison
volting out through its own demands.

(1981)

19

2.

Fireweed

Looseleaf poems

*gathered around the connections
of language, learning and
teaching: what we are taught
and not taught
and what we manage to learn
in spite of everything*

Driving Home

driving home from the mountains with mom and grandma
we're almost there just past Thrasher's corner
and the easy glide downhill along the curve of the creek
and all the trees holding in the warm dusk
I'm loose in the back seat, a kernel in a shell,
my ears, pitchers, taking in the words
sliding back and forth between the two.
I hear a complicated word hanging in the air, a string of beads
with several syllables, don't quite know what it means,
isn't a good word or a bad word, I can tell that,
but a new word, holding all kinds of mystery and complexity.
I want to reach out and cup it in my hands, am too sleepy
or maybe too stubborn to ask, "what does it mean?"
but puzzle it out, rolling the sounds in my mouth like acorns.
I get an edge on the word, it almost jells into place,
but just then headlights burn and mom says, "wish they'd
turn their brights off," flashing hers, "clickclick, clickclick"
and the word fades, I lose hold of its name, its possibilities,
it sinks back into the conversation.

I know this is at best how I learn, through the
beckoning pleasure of speech, how it spreads ripples out
through the night air, and we follow it, for the simple
sensual pleasure of that knowing,

a kite with a long translucent floating fin

the year I was Harriet
I could do math
and was bossy

that was third grade
and there were two Karens
so I turned into Harriet
who was my grandma
and my middle name.
chin thrust forward
I stood up in that room
and the numbers
clicked to attention
I wasn't fooled
by them anymore
their squeaks
their chalky tongues
their carrying on.
all that year, brassy,
I was wild horse, holding my own
reins loose, knees tough with scars,
taking the ground for granted.
my elbows stuck out to the sides,
my glasses gleamed with fake
diamonds and purpose.
I stuck my head under my desk
and ate grape jello raw
right out of the package,
then peered up, bloody purple.
when Mrs. English shrieked,
"oh lord what now?" I just
bared my bright teeth
in a weird, brave smile.

Mama says Florence

Mama says Florence
has such gorgeous flaming red hair!

Florence unsnarls my baby hair
I freeze on a highchair
waiting for the yank
but she unweaves each knot softly

What delicate bones Virginia has
my mother says, and those eyes!
always with pleasure, a dwelling on

Across-the-creek-Mary canters steady round her corral
weekends off from the library brings me soft-eared books,
patient, trains that colt, Akimbo
skims the corral, kicking up trouble, sorrel hair
flooding her thin shoulders

She never married but she carries her height well,
mother comments in a certain tone. I say,
Mary, you're so Tall, and she laughs,
but mama makes me take back what I meant as high praise.
Mary-slim-as-a-whip, you carry it well,
I canter with your generous laugh.

Oh that Sherry's got her mother's good looks, sighs mom.

And what of her own
fine dark hair puffed
above vulnerable forehead?

Her light sarcastic laugh/wide brim spilling
speckles and flecks/shadows of birds
over her skin/seared even through straw

She bends down weeding spicy pinks.

■

Mama said rainwater's softer, daughter

no words or names to see ourselves
girl   wife   old maid   divorcee   old lady
I couldn't even think the word   a sharp
breath in winter   the word

mouth sealed shut. blind date. strapped myself
into the right back seat. Patsy and the other unknown
kidding around in front

in the movie, with a couple, shadowy, stolid.
a young man comes up and says sweetly,
"would you like to be androgynous?"
"I don't know," I say nervously, "I'm still deciding."

no words. no women's menswear then. we sat over by the side
of the school, or streamed opposite to the rally,
or curved our hands round our stubborn breasts
and stood silent during the pledge.

Can you imagine doing what is absolutely unnatural?

in fact, I didn't choose to be a lesbian.
I only thought Shelley's face was the most beautiful.
we were eleven. we vowed to always stay
the same height and weight.

in fact, I choose to be a lesbian. after years of
running backwards, awkward. my ignorance and fear.
having no words to know what I felt.

no name for the long line of Margot's back. for the way
she magnetized the room. for the way she peeled
a grapefruit and ate each pale section in the summery
greenhouse of the dance studio. for the way I watched
her lean hands pulling the sections apart. for my thirst.

this eagerness, learning touch again,
body taut,
a shivering bow, "like a boy"

ah, she's a soft touch

Nostalgia Geranium was her Name

neon fish in their torn veils circle
ah the special on salamanders and trout this evening
trumpet flowers just a little wilted dear but elegant

your curls ruffled, here; let me smooth them, there. . .
and floating down darkened Liberty Street past vivid tvs
with ultra pink dancers streaming gauze
swimming toward us from their screens in the quiet shop

why, there she is again, leaning back slightly from the waist
slim in a long tight dress with a hint of bustle
her wrist flung up before her eyes, fingers finning out

   she sways a bit in the wind, dress on the line,
           and her hat is askew

"Really," I think, and tap her sharp on the wrist which
makes her jump. "Now look," I say, "See all those old
photos, they're frayed, here, you must take
this one, and this one," I smack them into her palm,
"and this one and this one. Now burn them."

I turn my back to walk up the hill and am spun by her wail
a long piercing cry that arcs up over the sleeping streets
cuts right through the shivering streetlamps and shatters
them out. as she, that geranium, stoops to retrieve her hat.

Irons in the Fire

Song for Merle

Both oars in the water
No feet on the ground
You and me in the hammock
Dancing all around

Honey tell me yr stories
Honey tell me yr worries
I've got a bee in my bonnet for you
I've got a singular sonnet for you

One time you woke me at midnight
One time you rocked me at noon
When I think of yr knees and so on
A shiver runs right up my spine

Two hawks up in the fir tree
Four arms wrapped all about
Two heads together
Singing some new joy out

The Fighter of Fires

The father is sulking on the steps, sleeves rolled up.
The summer day is fair. The children play in the fields,
amid milkweed pods and fennel in the headlong grass.

Mama's ready to go into town, standing before the mirror,
poufing her dark hair up above her forehead and
securing it with a comb. She's whizzing off again,
likes New York, the bustle.

Dad says, "You're off again. So take the goddam chicken
with you then. I'll be sitting here when you get back.
So take the goddam bird." She eyes his flushed angry face,
his set chin. He's picking apart a blade of grass.

Balanced on the sill, the charred roasting pot, lidded.
She's got a qualm or two, and bruises for evidence.
She'll edge up carefully to what he says, turning the words,
the tone. Her ears are tuned. The children line up
behind the hedge and peer through the leaves.

She stretches a hand out gingerly to lift the lid,
then leaps back and runs from it. Everyone else is running,
too, the whole field furious with leaves and scraps of cloth
and dust, because out of the pot has emerged the smooth
deadly back of a metal egg that cracks and rips, then
blows apart. It's a bomb. No food here. He did it.
The whole shed now in pieces suspended in air.

And I'm one of the kids, running, dashing, dodging
through the meadow, over the fence, into the woods, leap
the creek, down the path by the tracks, the cornpatch,
the neighbor field, with the horses running now too
at my side, and I'm sobbing and falling down into the
warm ground and picking up the sobs of my chest and
running with the pounding

Gasping Ma Ma where are you gone to Ma

Hush, says a big solid woman. Just hush. Your mama's gone now.
She's gone off to learn how to be a firefighter.
And she'll be back. Now you stay close and learn a few things
from me, and time won't stand still in its bare feet too long.
You settle down here now.

Then we fixed him, the bombdragger, womanhater, the measly mug, the
old geezer, ticker face, all the little kids tried to poison him
over and over, left the poison around in mugs and buckets and tubs
and rivers, but he never touched the stuff. Even when he fell
face down in the mud and had to straggle out soaked and shivering,
he kept his mouth shut tight around his teeth. So we called,
"hey hey where's the sheep run, ho, where's the pig roost, who's
the sulky prince?" And chased him and nattered him in little groups
of twos and threes, pins and needles wherever he turned. And the
neighbors looked away from him. He had tried to blow that woman away
and all for her floating free.

And finally one day, tears came to his eyes and he began to sob
and sobbed and sobbed until his body lay flat and smooth and exhausted.
Then we brought him something nourishing to eat.

And he ate. And he lived a long time in the town, fishing
and sat on his stoop and took care of the sheep. One day he died
at an old age. The woman was living nearby, with her children
and fought fire after fire, bravely, till no flames dared flame
but in the center of her hearth, the words of her breath,
the shine of her eye. And when the old man's funeral arrived, she
sat solemnly in his parlor, rocking, her feet crossed at the ankle
in firefighter's boots, and talked at length with her neighbors
of all the changes that had come about.

While her children ran in and out of the house and one of them
was writing a chronicle of the countryside which was laced
with the names of herbs and their uses—raspberry, mugwort,
slippery elm, angelica, fennel, fireweed, and the like.

■

Fireworks

it was never the fireworks we went for
but the massing of bodies in soft dark cloth
gathering, settling, the way everyone moved
in the same direction, speaking quietly in the
hush,
and waiting and staring out over the water,
it was never the fireworks we went for
but that long unanimous lifting ohhhhh
as the first light broke

Fireweed

I'm in a rowboat. I reach the shore of an island,
walk toward a fire, quick and bright. Take woodshingles,
hold them flat over the fire, warming my palms. As the
wood flames, I realize I'm dreaming about teaching.

Teaching this class is convincing people they have a right
to speak their minds. It is saying write like lightning
then judge. I see each new group caught in terror of form
as if that were the only question. I ask what holds you
back from writing and an older man says, "Verbs, verbs,
the past tense grips me." A woman says, "It is too easy,
didn't take hours, so it must be nothing." Who taught
us our images don't live and breathe?

Added to all this, that images are the livewire sparks
between opposites, a bridge that smokes between people.
And that those most pushed down have the most to say,
in images, shouts, actions, all just under the smooth
velour of the manufactured stories. Images leap out
of contradiction, blasting the true story into breath.

I'm in a field my father gardened. The garden is wild.
Deep in berries and long grass. Four people from my class
are here. We set up a table and chairs. We play cards
with a translucent deck. The cards, slips of plastic,
rest on our palms like windows. I draw a picture, though
I don't know how. The sketch outlines a fierce, strong
woman. Her short hair is dark and shining. Her face
is lined and spare. I try to fill in the cropped edge
of her hair where it meets her neck. I try again and
again to charcoal in the lines of her high cheekbones.
When I turn back toward the class, my arms overflow
with purple-red flowers from the Cascades called Fireweed.

Driving Through the Mountains at Night

we continued on into the mountains toward evening
each curve following the next in a practical line
we drove all the way through the night and slept our way
back to morning. you go through, not over, truly over,
that would be assuming too much about the mountains
about what is allowed and what is possible
you go through water and the lacy dark skim of trees
that tolerate the steady hum of the motor, only tolerate

conversation is like music on a long drive like this
while we all but the driver watch out through the window
at the outlines of trees and mountains against the sky
at the chalky shadows of higher peaks
phosphorescent under the moon   conversation proceeds
at an easy pace on a long drive like this
as if we are half asleep and our dreaming lives slip out
like moles and nudge around on the lawn, bending the grass
blades only slightly down and our paws damp from the mist

sometimes you are resting   between one pull-off and another
on a long drive like this   and the hands of your mother
or your friend   easy and resting on the wheel   with the
delicate veins moving their blood along peacefully and
forward   and your hands are like hers   on a long drive
and your brain content and humming   and the road
folding you in   and the talk singing out in the dark
and folding you in   and folding you in

3.

Here, Take My Words

For Harriet Pierce and Mary Brodine

Here, Take My Words

I prefer to believe that the last time we saw each other,
she rushed out of the house in a rage and hitchhiked home
to her shack.

But this isn't fiction. So I have to say that the last time
I say hello to that face, she looks past me to the wall and
I'm not her granddaughter any more, it can't matter to her anymore.

"Nabana," she says, "Nabana!" and I peel one.

. . . . .

Her skin shines down the resthome hall like a beacon.

She is naked from the waist up and her body gleams as if she is
a wet seal. Her breasts are longer and heavier than I remember
and seeming to fade, the nipples soft and undefined.
She strains forward from the straps that bind her to the chair,
shifting her weight back and forth. She says hello to my
mother but doesn't seem to see me.

"I'm hungry, don't you have a little something?"
        "Didn't they give you breakfast, mother?"
"I don't know, Mary. It isn't enough. Don't you have
a little something?"

We have two bananas in the paper sack, with two pairs of new
socks. . .with blue stripes. The blue stripes make me mad somehow,
they are so cheerful.

"Get your clothes back on now, mother. Here's your robe. Let's
put your clothes back on, now. Karen, find her other slipper. . .it's
lost." We talk of her in the third person as if she isn't there.

"Lost who? Who's lost?"

"Mother, we've lost your slipper. I've got to get your clothes together."

"Get me together. Then we can all be together fine," she snorts sarcastically.

Here it is under the bed. We put the fuzzy slipper on her hard claw foot, clenched and curved from no use.

"Karen's here," my mother says.
   "Where?"
"Right here," I say.
   "You don't look like Karen."

"Maybe you're remembering me when I was little."
   "I don't recognize you."
"I recognized you right away, Grandma."
   "You did? That's good. How are you?"
"Oh, I'm fine."
   "Well, I wish I was fine. Then we'd all be fine together."

She is picking at her buttons, trying to slip out of her robe again.
"Mother, don't take your clothes off," says my mother.
   "Why not?"
"Because you'll catch cold," I lie, feeling foolish. The room is very warm.
   "Because they don't like it," my mother says, more honest.
We watch her hands roving like two determined animals over the robe.
Her fingers light on a corner of it and she pulls it up.
   "Give me a look at this, what does it say?"
"Grandma, you can't read your robe and you can't eat your socks."
She almost laughs at this. Then she looks hard at me and points,
"Give me the little girl in there. Give me the little girl."

She changes the subject. "I'd like to get back to what I had."
   "You had a lot."

"I did?" She brightens, thinking maybe of wished for land, the ship come
in, the lucky break, the good job that leered around the corner.
      "Yes, you had a lot. You're the strongest person I know."
"I'm glad to hear that," she says and her eyes focus on mine. We stare
unsmiling at one another for a minute. I imagine that something goes
between us, unspoken yet solid, yet, I'm not sure, maybe it's just that
I want some signal from her.

"Get me out of here," she says, pulling at the straps.
      "Where would you go then, if you could leave?"
"Oh, I'd be going toward home. Get me a phone."
      "Grandma, I can't, but who would you call?"
"I'd call for something useful."
      "Well, they'll bring your lunch soon," says my mom. "That's useful."
"I don't want lunch, then I'll be like a lake."

I take her socks out and print on them with a marker. H. Pierce in red
letters. She watches curiously. "Can you sign my socks?"

A nurse comes in to say hello. "Gee Harriet, you're not talking much. . ."
the nurse turns to us. "Usually she just chatters and chatters. Gee,
Harriet, you're not saying much. See you later. . ." There's a long silence.
Then my grandmother looks at me and extends her hand, palm up.
"Here," she says, "Take my words."

I realize she has been hurt by the woman's words. My mother says,
"Oh don't pay attention to that woman darlin."
"Why?"
      "Because, mother, it doesn't matter, it's alright."

It is time for us to leave because we can't stand to stay any longer.
An hour seems like a long time. "Goodby," she says, politely, formally,
to me, and as we leave, she is slowly shedding her clothes,
like soft, wilting leaves.

(1978)

43

Grandmother Harriet Pierce.
(Left) Karen and Harriet.

Her Stubborn Spirit

Last night's dream: scrabbling through boxes of rummage in the basement
of my house where Grandma used to live. Old sofa stuffed with
hay and fireplace choked with ashes. I step through the cellar,
each door smaller, a miniature of upstairs. Then I find Grandma's
room, windows staring out at ground level. You can see inside
the earth, how everything lifts up for the sun, even the roots,
even the stones, even the child watching Grandma comb her
silverstreaked hair.

It's hard to absorb her death. She's so distant.
Where's the proof? She just vanished, leaving a blank
screen with no images, only scraps of half-finished thoughts.

Make reservations, call work, straighten my room, call Mom.
We always knew Grandma intended to live forever. "Yeah,"
I say, "the older she got the more she believed in reincarnation,
nothing was gonna do her in."

My plane lifts through the blue, far-sighted morning.
There are the folded bones of the mountains where she'll drift down.
"She never liked the ocean," says Mom, "but she loved the Cascades."
And besides she always was like a volcano.

A small white plane suspends far below over the foothills.
Cremation. $250.00. Poor woman's funeral.
The only thing the poor get that's better.
I'd rather burn clean than settle in a box, anyday.
Does her stubborn spirit arc out from her bones
in one sudden leap or in fragments of language,
and dream, all the unfinished business?

. . . . .

Mother and I talk a lot, slowly, now and then, all weekend.
She feels stupid, guilty, because she's numb.
"That's shock, the body taking care." We say, not "she was. . ."
but ". . .she is." Her scratchy voice still slaps me between my
shoulder blades, she glares, then calls me honey.

Phone the *Detroit News* where she worked forty years ago.
Mom wants an announcement there. She organized in that shop.
Call the funeral home. (all this against a tremendous lethargy—
Grandma, stop nudging with your snappy, pushy words, do this,
do that, leave me alone, damn it)

Writing the obituary. . .
"Harriet Miller, born 1897, married to David Pierce."
I argue about this, "why put that in, she divorced him."
"She didn't divorce him, Karen, they were *separated*."
Worked at the *Detroit News*, moved to Seattle, then Clearview.
Survived by daughter, Mary Brodine, and granddaughter, Karen.

A lot left out. Prison reform work, her radicalism, many jobs,
the McCarthy HUAC trials. The time she sent maggots from the
prisoners' bread in a jar to the governor. The poems she wrote
in spiral notebooks. The recipes scrawled from her years as
a cook, trailed by agents from one restaurant to another,
fired again and again.

How she held together in that time. The clothes she sewed,
copied by memory from fancy stores downtown. Feet flying
on old shuttle machine.

Mom said she'd like more of Grandma's radical days in the obit, but "some people around here wouldn't understand. And it's important to say she was married because they insulted her at the pension place, said she'd just been 'co-habiting' with my dad, wasn't really his widow, couldn't get his veteran's benefits." A lot coming to her she never got. "Maybe at first they did live together—her a young girl orphaned at 16, him 15 years older—him Irish Catholic—and his family hating her because she was Jewish. He took care of her. But I know they got married, the records just burned."

No rights. Not property, not marriage, both refused, hand in hand.

"Why didn't she write more?" Mom wonders. "She had great ideas but never got them down on paper much. Except a few poems and articles." "I don't know," I say, "Maybe she didn't have enough confidence. . .having to quit high school and finish later. Maybe just being a strong, ambitious woman without a feminist movement, a loud-mouthed radical woman among men."

"Oh no," Mom disagrees. "The men respected her. They didn't respect their wives, but they knew better than to cross her. She'd tear them up and down if they said anything bad about women. She could talk circles around them, cut right to the heart of an argument, like a good knife. And she never kept it a secret that she considered herself a little superior to the men."

Grandma wanted to see photos while she was in the rest home. Mom took in pictures of all of us, but Grandma just wanted to look at herself; *that* handsome woman. A Leo, imperious, sometimes insensitive, a powerhouse, and sure, beautiful, too.

"Huh, remember, Karen, that story about when I was little and your grandma and me were in a big old hotel on the third floor and she was talking, as usual, and then all of a sudden, her voice went wooooooo fainter and then nothing. Silence. She had opened a door, curious, and stepped into the dark, went sliding down the laundry chute, ended up in the basement in a heap of towels and sheets."

"Oh, and when I was sick and she wouldn't stay away from the hospital. A couple of times she commandeered cabs, hopped out and dashed into the hospital, then got lost on the elevator, kept riding up and down, up and down."

Both of us laugh, hard, remembering. How after she couldn't drive anymore, she'd hitch, and tell a tall tale to whoever picked her up. Something about how terrible Mom treated her, so there'd be some strange woman with a carload of kids and Grandma climbing out, thanking her sweetly, while the woman stared in the window accusingly at us.

She didn't always hitch either, sometimes hiked, her red purse full of bills (always ready for the crash, don't trust those bankers). At 80, she'd hike all the four miles to Mom's house, in a determined one two, right down the yellow line.

. . . . .

I've fallen down into sleep through an elevator that won't stop no difference between travelling up and down, wait to crash or fall, but finally simply stop. no bump. just stop.

Clamber out into an enormous basement, dark, just a faint glimmer from a roaring furnace. Creep through, bumping into furniture. Over there is the furnace man. Can't see him, but he'll get you if he can. Shovel in the fuel and stay away from me, old man. Don't come near me.

Out the window I go, set at ground level, breaking up
through the earth, flower bed, daisies and thorns,
sun stinging my eyes, here I am.

Wish I knew more about her life—as a radical, an
independent working woman.

I ask if there's anything left of Grandma's
and Mom says, "well I kept her old writing desk down in
her room in the basement, where she lived when you were small. . .
You know, near the furnace where the window is at ground level
and everything streams toward the sun."

The Piano with Wings

1.

Upright. Weber. 1899. Shiny dark finish with yellow silk lining, carved inlay. Real Silk, my mother said.

It was so hot in St. Louis, she said, and I'd practice hours and hours a day; it was me and the piano in the rented room and the sweat pouring off my body and onto the keys.

The piano came west all the way to Seattle, mother's hand resting on the cool shining skin. All the way west in a piano bar, gliding the rails over the highest Cascades. She thought Mt. Rainier was a dream at first, impossible. Up all forty steps to the house on Beacon Hill. She got married, then played the piano till her stomach wouldn't fit under the keyboard anymore. Then I was born. She said I screamed everytime she touched the keys, even in passing.

In summer you could lean against the side and the whole length of your body cooled. You could press your full weight against the bulk, and it would never move. We kept secrets in under the felts and dampers, old coins in a jar, the locket her mother gave her.

She kept the piano on an inner wall away from the draft, near my room, so her practicing and teaching hummed in my ears. All the years, my father's jealousy and our lack of money kept her from studying, she'd chew at the same exercises, the intricate bars, with a stumble, a stutter, the driving up toward perfection, the stopping short at the same place, the chords battering the walls, metronome racing ahead. Her face stiffening as she stood in the kitchen listening to him lift the lid, plunk a few casual chords down hard on the keys.

Finally, she began to study again, with a fine teacher, and the long hours
of practice flowing and lifting, springout, blossoms, the river of chords,
her emotions released. Shoulder. Keys. Hands short and strong, the
veins blue. Body leaning into the sounds.

Keys wearing down, the ivories chipping, her gold tooth.
The pillow she used because the bench wasn't high enough.
Her soft skin and the scarred grace of the piano.

I walked in one summer to find she'd run from the tub,
humming to catch the phone and perched naked on the piano bench,
skin flushed, face cupped into the mouth and ear of the phone,
free hand resting on the keys. So serene in the muted light
of the window shaded by wisteria.

And after the stroke, still she played, haltingly,
beginning again, with one good hand.
"I never lost the feeling, just the ability to move.
I could feel the sounds running through my veins."

That piano so heavy, yet it moves, no one could lift it
yet it slides down the steps, no one could contain it,
yet it rides in a truck, no one could own it, and it
lives now with a student who loved my mother
and learned from her.

2.

I sold it
heart of the house
see the work, the carved wood
the piano stood
in the center of the light
she said, Play it Play
original wood
new dampers
concert tone
perfect C
oh could she play

piano tuner asks
why out in the sticks?
so much training
St. Louis Institute
she faced that piano night and day

had a bad marriage
had me
raised me up
then got free

piano with wings
sold now gleams
in a mobile home
with sweet Theresa
and the deaf cat
who used to curl
in Mama's lap.

the piano needed
to be played
and shook
another husband up,
at that.

get in practice, Theresa,
friend and student
for all you must do
with practice
you will gain strength.

Karen's mother,
Mary Pierce Brodine.
(Right) Mary
with baby Karen.

No Storm So Rough You Don't Wake

In memory of Mary Brodine
September 20, 1981

No warning, only indrawn breath of ocean,
undertow raking the beach,
rush out, rush out, drawing breath with it
sieve of the sand sifted through and clean

Long sigh out and remnants of kelp and shells
gleam wet, beached up

A woman stands upright facing the water,
pitches full length forward

Driving north toward rain with Merle
in the night I fall, lurch awake.

Taking my time to get there.
Don't want to. Face it.
Don't want to look. Look.
Silver maple shining so soft,
each burnished leaf gathering light.
It's a cat, a cat, fur afire, in the trees,
a fierce prism burning in the leaves.

I will wake her. She lies in my arms now.
She died defending someone.
Flamed up, now lies limp in my arms.
I dip my fingers in milk, hold them to her mouth.
She begins to stir, to wake, to drink.

Mother met it, sitting up, dressed
at six in the morning.
She met it knowing, if not willing.

They carried her away to burn her.
In a long sack cloth.
Only her sweater thrown over the chair
still shaped to the soft lines of her body.
Only her i.d. and glasses.
Only her cats crying for food.
The rest of her scattered over the mountains.

For her I buy red flowers, candles, wine, cake.
And prop up all the pictures of her. Polish
the piano. Sweep the floor and build a fire.
Her students will play and I will read.
It is night and raining again.
People begin to arrive.

I close the door after her last friend leaves.
Thought I couldn't face this.
Having to builds muscles.

Merle and I buy rubber gloves,
Ajax, paper towels, sponges.
We wash and scrub and sweep and rinse.
At night I sit near the fire
and burn and sort and burn.

Each day a new list, garage sale, taxman, cats,
friends, obituary, property, piano, mother, mother
rocking chair, books, photos, the old painting
of peasant women, grandma, mother,
granddaughter
somewhere in Italy in gold-brown light.
That's all I want to keep.

I will never go to the hospital again, she said.
No way to live, helpless.

She met it, sitting up on the couch
where all her conversation and business
of living occurred. Her cane nearby.
And she let go. One minute, she hung on
facing it, and the next minute
everything in the room was changed.

She streams out with this first torrential rain
cars wading up to their hoods in flood
lights glimmering below the surface
and sinking to a steady, watery beam

The creek fills, the house leans into the rain,
I hang in the wet sky above the trees.
Water spills over, swells in my chest.

No storm so rough you don't wake.
Mother, you don't wake.

"We'll remember Mary," says her friend Tim,
"by the day that thunder shook the sky
and the creek washed out the bridge.
Remember Mary by the cloudburst
that took everyone by surprise."

Three Letters

1. From My Grandmother to My Mother

Detroit, March 29, 1942

Dearest Mary,

Your note was most welcome. . .

The Labor Board hearing to determine our bargaining unit has been in session for a whole week. Startling disclosures have been made, and at last, the *Daily News* has doffed its paternalistic mask to reveal the ogre which was there all the time.

Thursday night we worked getting out a mailing until the wee hours, at last, our forces had diminished to three.

Friday night we were tired as hell, result we didn't do so well, but fortunately Paul W. came over when he quit work at midnight. He'd had some stimulant on the way over, and started off and finished in high.

It was then 5 am and I was expected to take charge of a ream of handbills. I had spent the evening pledging by phone. I went to the Guild's room, slept two hours, had a shower, and betook myself with the stack of handbills to the front door of the *News*. When I got home last night at 2 o'clock, I simply flopped on the bed, fully dressed and went to sleep. We had a good meeting at 3:30 this afternoon and I went to one of the janitor's homes to track down some evidence for tomorrow's hearing.

My sociology class finishes Wednesday. I'm supposed to turn in several papers and tomorrow night is the deadline. The subjects are: The Negro Problem, Propaganda, the War and the Future, Personality Maladjustment. I could speak on all these sufficiently well to satisfy the instructor but it seems very difficult to write when so many things are happening to distract from concentrated effort.

Don't worry about my not getting enough rest. I have never felt better.

All my love,
Mother

2. Letter to My Mother

San Francisco, July 26, 1984

Dear Mom,

What a week, everyone running in high gear, the whole city, in
throes of convention. Condensed collision of Democrats, strikers,
press, Moral Majority, picketers, cops. We're strung all week
on the tightwire of picketlines, threat of cops looming on horseback.

Here's a story you'd like. During the '34 General Strike in San
Francisco, people padded their hats with paper. Sure, someone
says, they'd bop each other on the head and keep stuffing in the
paper till it didn't hurt. Then they were ready for the picketline.

It's a warm day but we layer ourselves in coats and hats. They may
just arrest us for how we look. Tom in fedora, Ro in rainhat, Nell
in Chinese construction hat, Merle and Pat in Greek fishermen's caps,
Nancy in CWA hat. Off to fight the Klan.

I'd like to tell you about the openness, the energy of the city this
week, people coming up, old and young pointing to our signs, saying,
"Who's on strike now? Where's the Klan marching? I want to be there
to kick their ass out of town." Mr. Rivera, the printer next door
looks relieved each night as we troop back, "Not arrested yet, huh?"

Don't get behind a horse. . .or in front of one, either. A cop nearly
runs Nell down, then reins the horse in, wheels, and Tom and I try
to hold it at bay with picket signs: cardboard and words.

At a signal, the cops charge on their cycles and horses, knocking
people down, beating one medic to the ground. We see the billy club
thud, thud.

The crowd chants, "The whole world is watching." It's rush hour
and seems as if the whole city has converged here. . .from the older
salesclerks at Macy's, most of them women of color, to the dazed
punkers, hair spikey, wandering like small bands of porcupines
into the headlights of cops on motorcycles. And all of us shoved
back onto steep sidewalks by steely rows of cops, with the press
streaming in, staring through their lenses, like detached, curious fish.

Late at night again, dragging home. . .another hate letter from the
Klan? Not this time, it's a letter to you, Mom, still trickling
in, forwarded from all the good samaritans of the world: ACLU,
PAWS, Friends of the Earth, Concerned Scientists, Gloria Steinem,
the envelopes still arriving.

Since I'll be in the neighborhood, I guess I'll drop by. . .see how the
house is doing. . .hope the new people left the trees, those thick
cedar branches that kept you cool in summer, warm in winter.

At night, in dreams, we range around the city. . .in and out of clumps
of people congregating on street corners. . .everywhere, debates,
information, surging like electricity.

While at the hall, leaflets roll continuously off the mimeo. . .
bright pages we reach out with, "They're free! Take a look.
No more lesser evil politics! Stop the rightwing!" We plow on,
at full speech, dancing out in front of the streaming crowds
dealing leaflets like quick cards or landing birds.

One Saturday picket at Macy's Department Store grows till it
thunders in a blockbusting crowd around the store. Managers
stare down from the roof ten stories high, the crowd points up,
jeers, "Jump! Jump!" The line surges around and around, spills
off the sidewalk, the chants pulling into one immense roar,
outraged and exuberant.

3. Letter to Meridel Le Sueur

San Francisco, January, 1981

Dear Meridel,

You've written to me a couple of times—handfuls of words swimming
along the page. I've written back. And here's another letter,
as much a frame for all I want to say today, as a letter. I've
been wanting to write a whole piece: a form unfolding in my mind
like a long warm swatch of material, not sectioned. And myself
insisting, "But what's the content?" Took a friend to say,
"Can't desire for a certain form be talking about content?
That you want to write a piece about connections, no gaps or rips?"

We all need examples, the ones who go before us, speaking out.
You are such a person, your ideas streaming back through the lives
of many women and men.

I never wanted to bear children, but a daughter, half-grown, to
talk to, that would be ok. I would have named her Resolve.
And I think how in a group, there are the older and younger,
the bonds forming, the examples set, the tumultuous ones
leaping forward when you least expect. A group, an organism,
a fluid, energetic atom, resolving through collective theory
and action—how fragile that can seem, but how strong it is.
No matter how anyone tries to deny us or leave us or stamp
us out, if our words and actions have integrity, we will persist.

I read your stories because they are history and necessity
all at once. In each paragraph live women of irony, bitter wisdom,
strength. And inside my hands, words line up, horses at the gate,
their large eyes shut, skin twitching in the heat and dust,
the pressure builds—hunger for symbol and image, hunger
for the mark of change.

Believing in that change. . .

But I'm no hopeless optimist. I'm a hopeful realist. Someday
we'll have a real celebration for all of us, not having to stuff
full, scared we won't get enough—enough food, enough love,
enough money, enough sleep.

If the cat can lie with her whole body relaxed like that, why
can't we? Because the mikes are lollygagging around with no
amps, because the childcare workers haven't been found,
because the computer robot gets overloaded and walks right off
the screen, it says so in the manual.

Everything is manual. Lifting chairs for the meeting, chopping
zucchini, typing minutes, plumping pillows, rubbing her shoulders,
speaking magic markers in big red letters: STOP THE KLAN,
ABORTION RIGHTS, UNITED WE STAND.

There are men who lean off balance from their edges, who say,
"I want to see her dead." I have a bat by the bed just in case.
It's a possibility I want to meet with all the right tools.

I am dragging her back, the slight young girl. All the grim
eyed ones watch, stuffed into their suits. They have such
cold eyes and hands. They say, "give up your bodies as ransom
to God, you can't decide to be gay," and drag her off, screaming.
But I won't let it happen. I grab her waist, her hands, and
pull her back.

Everyday the determination to grow stronger. . .

Typesetting Friday, my fingers rained the words out tiny and
perfect, clear pebbles at the floor of the stream like Shelley
and me sliding down the river on our bellies over boulders
velvety with moss and the current took us and we didn't steer
but ended up in the shallows with all the river's direction
lifting and warming and filling us out.

The other night I saw hundreds of minute horses, red sea
horses, bobbing in the ocean, all our words, our lives
streaming up from the deep—raw, skinned, nerves exposed,
but swimming and bobbing, red apples, banners, clay, blood,
the color to revive this planet. And Meridel, if your words
swim up and are sustained and move us, then I know my
words can do that too.

Meridel, Hien Luong, Clara Fraser, Nellie Wong, so many women
shouting out we belong to the whole red-stained, cloud-rimmed
earth and brimming oceans and the light belongs to us all,
knowing the earth must be turned, baring the rich dark soil,
knowing we must take power all together
in the long run

for we are the left feathers of the left wing
fierce dappled sleek span
the whole body depends upon

4.

Left
Feather

Visible Agenda

Here's our life, I mean, here's our line

       pursuing the political angel

the snow of the pages falling around us mimeomimeo

        taking off bumpily in the bargeplane
        you know I'm scared of heights
        my palms even get sweaty when I watch Stuntman

        little pig, her feet dangling from the hoist,
        held up by her belly, hooves wildly treading air

so here we are plunked wildly up down, up down
in this creaky convertible with wings
it's an outdoor cafe, too, with snackbar
and a couple of umbrellas for shade

next we touch down in a military installation
with guards marching about in ominous uniform gray
no way out but this wheezy shuttle bus

every night I dream airplanes, paperclips, press releases,
scruffy wildeyed cats, traffic tickets, agendas

trying to keep an overview
the whole caboose.
we can see it all, too, through patchy clouds,
as we cling, queasy, to the edge of the barge,
we can see the waves of clear air riding up at us
and the fields and cities
and people going to work.

the political angel hovers near the mimeo machine
or over the phone, taking notes. she speaks out,
malicious, critical, and has visions

and watches tv, searching for the perfect mirage

and beelines toward the sharp, true belief

and always wanted to be a standup comic.

(1983)

Two Pages of the Book

1.

Snow field

Blank page

Darkroom red and slumbrous, paper slick

and winding through the processor to nudge

my hands now articulate with words

Blackberry stains on scratched arms

warm berries thunk thunk into the pail then no sound

and the heavy pleasant weight of the filling pan

Shape, shape gathering

in the dark folds of the sleeping mind

The idea, the letter, the word, the labor

that puts it into action. Riverbank edge

of alphabet spilling over into song

The dream of the page shaped by words

The dream of the book

punctuated by the turning page

Thought that binds us together

2.

Well, you know, she said, those lurid shades
of color xerox? Tropic polaroid sunset
or maybe 2,000 milligrams big orange vitamin C?
Neony. Peony. Anyway, that was the color
of the doublepage spread of the book.

And get this, there's a rollercoaster of letters
chained together with the peaks and dips
and steep dizzy turns of the words all electric
and the flashbulbs snapping off and on,
doubletime. A b S Z D T   jumping rope
hot pepper   Flashing traffic signals
Sirens and horns beeping

Yeah, well, she sighed. I guess the design was
a little too flashy.

      Simplify. Simplify.

■

(1985)

No One Immune

1. The Rightwing in the Morning with Coffee

They've sneaked into the water supply
some deliberate plutonium, all New York City
swallows and this is no different
than workers in the California fields
breathing pesticides through their skins

Reagan explains graphics
of doorknobs and steering wheels
dusted with translucent KGB poison
that American ambassadors touch.
Of course you can't see it,
he says, but it's there,
mark my words.

While the nation stares, puzzled,
at a naked doorknob clothed
in the Emperor's new dust.

2. Sickness Slept in Us

*Seattle Times, 11/11/84: "The West German Health
Ministry said it was considering legislation calling
for prison terms for AIDS victims who know they have the
disease and continue having sex."*

It was a time when sickness slept in us waiting
It was a time when birds dove through slick oil
and came up without feathers
a time when no one was immune

Are you now
or have you ever been
a member of those
who face the days with no natural defense?
who face a slow and certain death?
diagnosed, the new lepers
under wrath of god.

Can they lock us all up?

3. A Scapegoat is One Bearing Blame, Falsely

Driving through soft rain, flaming autumn
edging into winter, north toward mountains
past Woodinville, Clearview, to Snohomish

Highways widen, pushing up to doors like rivers
green our valley, now engulfed in tires,
spare parts, farms replanted in metal, woods gone.

Up through the sleepy towns, loosening their
hold on the land, tossing up utilitarian bridges,
fast food stands.

Wandering into a second hand store
all sleek old homey wood
face to face with a placard
bold as everyday:
a placard of ceramic pins, pasty peasants,
the matter-of-fact words: "Nazi Party Pins"

I confront the shopowner, she mutters
pre-war Germany, Harvest Bounty, picking up the towns
from hard times, these pins rewards
for jobs well done. I point out Jews, gays,
socialists, millions killed, her mouth drops,
a slammed door.

Nazis in Snohomish.

4. Bones

There is a procession
There is a march
up from the sodden grassy banks
of the Green River
There is a march, a procession
up from the flooding waters
of the river where forty women
were murdered and dumped one by one.
One by one, after another, the women
return. The ones who are known
by name, the anonymous too.
The women who are missing, feared
dead. They drag themselves up
from the currents of the river.
The sisters who left in the morning
and never returned. The daughters
who vanished with never a phone call.
The women who by force of circumstance
or force of a gun, climbed into a stranger's car
at midnight or at noon, on the street
or in a shopping center and drowned
in the cold grasp of the terrorist.
These are the women filed in the detective's desk:
Bones 1, Bones 2, Bones 3.
Their teeth clack in the cold waters
of the river. Their shoulder blades
scrape and gleam. Bones 4, Bones 5, Bones 6.
They drag themselves out of the waters and
march, these disappeared, these lost women
down the avenue of the homeless in Pioneer Square,
through the suburban yards of the outlying districts.
Bones 7, Bones 8, Bones 9, like pale long trees rattling,
calling out his name. To find him. And we will.

(1985)

By Fire or by Water

1. February 1986

Dreams this terrible week.

Su and I are standing on an open porch waiting for people to
arrive. In every direction, a pure and fierce and gentle
snow is falling.

I'm dancing a kind of waltz-polka, faster, faster, till I
spin off from my partner, off balance, careening.

A tiny dog yaps at my heels, harassing, covered with seaweed.

won't let me BE.

Someone turns a waterhose full in my face, washes
me down concrete steps. In the dream I think,
"What did I do to deserve this?"

. . . . .

Some people act a little funny now, awkward about cancer—
I try to put them at ease with jokes. At times,
the anxiety rises in me like a flood.

. . . . .

The dr. says that once you have cancer, you are followed
by the medical profession for the rest of your life.

. . . . .

Wading through brush in the night, a man is following me.
I am not sure if this is by chance or if he menaces.
I turn to study his face. I whip my hands through the air
cutting at the brush to threaten him with how fierce I am.
He keeps following. I keep watch, beating at the brush,
wake, gasping. His face is young, square, somewhat
twisted, watching me.

I have seen his face.
He has seen my strength.
Who will win?

2. March 1986

When I was a kid someone would say,
ok, what would you choose, death by fire or water?
Pragmatic, I would never play that game. Now I have to.
A new twist, the bribe is life. Life by fire, death
by percentage, life by water, drowning
all your cells just enough.

Remission is disappearance for the time being.
Cure is death by other causes.

My chances for recurrence are 35% without chemo,
half that, with. A clear choice.
Till you add barbarities of treatment. Would you
prefer to chance diabetes or heart failure,
dizziness or seeing halos round the moon?

I've never been the least religious.
Now they're tossing halos round my neck like horseshoes,
and I'm the pole, no angel, stiff and afraid,
arm protective of the missing breast.

What will happen when I swallow the poison?
Which poison should I choose?

Someone flips a coin and here I stand in my body,
one more gamble, one more statistic.

I'm like a boy on one side, a woman on the other.
Doesn't bother me so much, reminds me of running wild
and lithe through the woods like a colt.
What bothers me is I may lose my lashes
through which I look, shaded and protected,
at the world.

The dr. says he's biased toward research.
I've got another bias.
The dr. says he can't say what he would advise
if it were his wife or daughter or even himself.
Because he's not in my position.
But what are imaginations for?

Too many times I have imagined my mother, wrestling
with her tardy, errant heart, anchored to that couch
by a failing muscle. Still she came back,
dragging half her body at the leash,
into determined movement and life.

3. April 1986

Trying to guide a horse and a lion
to safety, yarn about their necks,
hands tangled in their manes.
The animals are wild,
want to wander through the woods,
directionless, but we must go
toward home. Rough, make-shift tools,
the wild animals of the body.
Vigilance, consciousness, the ability
to fight. Understanding
in order to fight.

. . . . .

An evil woman kept changing shape.
She kept striking when I turned my back.
When I looked again, she had taken
all the tires off my car.

I knew it was her because she wore
One earring, icy blue, shaped like a
wind chime, irregular, jagged.

I faced her down.
We stared at one another.
I knew I couldn't look away.
This was a contest and I must not
even blink. We stared and stared
and finally, she changed into a
yolk-like substance and disappeared
into water, dissolved.

I had won, for this moment.

. . . . .

Trying all angles, everything I can think of,
not giving up, keeping steady in the assault
of the chemo that drains your energy out your
feet till you can't move. I fight the chemo
more than the cancer.

I don't trust in my weapons entirely.
The cell model helps, but it is abstract,
a picture, distant.

The reality is very complex and my mind clamors
to alter it into something concrete:
wicked witches, lions and horses, seaweed dogs,
men stalking me, and me, always
turning, straining to see, to see and to
engage in whatever fight is required

4. May 1986

Here, on that new strange plain
where my left breast is no longer
where the angry scar blanches out
to a thin reminder
Here, my heart is closer now
to my lover's ear, listening
to the sun lazing its warm palm
on my pale skin, closer now
to the traffic blare
to shouts of street people
to the rasp of each day,
the rough, practical tones.
My heart is closer now.
Hear its steady, stubborn drum.

(1986)

Casino Window

Standing at the window in the hotel room of the casino,
she saw the mountains looming, clear and acute.

Acute as this knowledge that her body was deserting her,
weakening into a stranger, a machine for making pain, unaccountable.
Still, she watched, with intense curiosity and intense hilarity,
the scene six stories below: the proceedings of the bridal party.

It was a bright mountain day, not yet the expected summer,
buffeted by a maverick northwest wind. The pastel clothes of
the guests seemed about to fly off. The flimsy arch sprigged
with flowers toppled and the attendants carried it off to obscurity.
The silver chalice of wine leaped into the air, and
drenched the minister.

The guitarist began to play (or seemingly) the wedding march.
She could see his hand and mouth working, but the wind took the sound.
All the guests flew into their chairs and craned their necks to see
the Bride billowing in a white parachute and anchored by several
desperate bridesmaids, who steered her down the pink runway
like a lavish, wayward ship.

The procession wafted forward, picking up the bride's father
and the groom, and swept toward the minister, who was struggling
to keep the pages from whipping off the Bible.

And the ceremony began, as she began to lose
interest, anchored only slightly in her own
gown, her bathrobe loose on the left side
where the breast was gone. She shivered in the sharp
wind, thinking of the bride tugging at her moorings
and of the avalanche of coins below,
flooding down into the depths of the casino
like a million silver fish.

(1987)

The Foolish Girl

Who are you, shadow, standing
still at the edge of the road?
I'll tell you of a foolish girl.
Who swooped about in a cape.
Who tied her fingers in knots
then combed them out with her long hair.
Who rushed headlong, losing things.

With such tough knees,
she knew that time would
heel to her quick pace.
She'd defy it, put it off,
and like her grandma,
slowly age into a hawk.
She thought the weak were weak
and feared their glance
would nix her luck.

Now dusk is more dear
and the faces of her friends.
She wants to memorize their bones
their laughter ringing out,
so strong, so sure.

And she grieves
for what is gone
and tries to nurse the fear
the bruise, the scar,
the stone cold truth,
the fist, the knot
that binds the rib
pounding at her heart
let me in, let me in.

She wants to weld her self
with scarlet veins
to the rickety cart
and drive on.

◼

(1987)

They Outlawed Touch

They outlawed touch between those of the same body,
no twins, no sisters, no friends, no neighbors

an oddity, the way I wash my hair, the way
        I bare my teeth?

get used to that word, perverse
you might as well get used
        to spit in your face

and know pacific as an ocean
        just some innocent ocean

        get used to flaunting
        your fists

reach across wall, ice, lock, myth
across lies we don't exist

while a candidate swears on a Bible he's no queer

I never knew what I was till I knew my name.
Dyke.

Lesbiana, the young girls jeer
and I know there must be one among them
swinging her skirts brashly
hearing her own name,
seeing herself
in me,
and I have loud names for this,
burnt kiss, singe
risk, pride
stronger tendon
tender
grin
fist hand human natural animal hand.

(1978)

Censorship

1. The Words

All my life, the urgency to speak, the pull toward silence.
Embodied in the two sides of the family; like a tree without a mouth,
my Swedish father, bottled up and bursting out in mean words,
or averting his eyes, he goes back in the house, he shuts the door,
he wants to feed us berries and fish and watches us talk and laugh
and our joy is reflected in his eyes, but he can only watch
as if we are a painting. And my mother and grandmother, Jewish,
overflowing with words, loving to talk about people, never can I
rival their stories—to laugh with but never at, the amazing quirks
of neighbors and friends.

One ear tuned to the strungtight wires of father's hands as he
picks raspberries. We are singing, "I'll take the high road
and you take the low road," he rolls the berries off the tall
bushes into a coffee can, while I eat the berries from the lower
vines. We sing but we don't talk.

Inside the house, in the cool, intimate kitchen, mother and
grandmother have been talking all afternoon. I hunch under the
table, scratching my name on the bare wood with a stubby pencil.
They are laughing and a chair scrapes and a cup clinks as mother
pours more coffee. I love their talk but I know how often it
crosses the border between relaxation and direction: "Karen go get
me a good head of lettuce from the garden," so I listen but I
hide under the table to listen in peace.

As to my own words, this will take awhile; no one could rival
my grandma, so I must wait till she's out of earshot to hear
myself think. But my mother and me, we talk back and forth; from
her I learn the company of words, the clarity of faces turned
together in interest, focused through speech.

And when I see her words muffled or stopped mid-sentence or
slapped back in her face with derision, or simply not begun,
I know the first rule of censorship, the shades drawn, the
expression dropping down into bitterness.

The first rule of censorship is a woman cramped in the arid grid
of economy and home, family and duty, powerless, held in, stopped
short. And the second rule is that in a hundred small ways, she
resists and then all at once when I am eighteen she bursts out
to live alone, to say whatever she wants. So I learn to follow
her way and speak out too.

2. Smuggling Books Across the Border

This time the censorship was a cop car floating along the Oregon coast.
We didn't see it at first, incognito colors and just blinking its
parking lights slowly. So that cop followed us for miles and kept
inventing mistakes till they came to 94 dollars. We were all quiet
and nervous, he barricaded our car in the driveway with his, for
three of us being Asian.

The ghost of his car followed us all the way home. In the unemployment
office they are teaching people in groups how to fill out the forms.
It will take two unemployment checks to pay that ticket and just glad
the cop didn't look in the trunk where the socialist books were packed.

A long time ago my mother put socialist books in the trunk.
Someone called on the phone to tell me, five years old,
"Your parents are commies. We're going to get you."
I hung around my dad all day, silent and scared because I thought
if I told him, then it would come true, saying it would make it
come true.

Clara sits late at night talking about censorship in the '50s
and sneaking pamphlets across the Canadian border in her baby's
diapers. "That was the fattest baby you ever saw." In that same
era, my mom was sitting in the kitchen saying things under her
breath, afraid my dad would explode.

They are banning more books now than during the Cold War.
While they print stereotypes of our lives. We watch caricatures
vaguely resembling ourselves giggle and simper on the screen.

But they can't shut us up. Memory drags out of us kicking and
screaming, bursting like pomegranate seeds, tart and succulent.
At work, we stack slabs of dynamite, wrapped in butcher paper.
We hoist each slab up delicately while the boss watches from a
distance; the paper around the explosive unfolds into a cloth,
a sheet against the wind, all these words to live in, swim in,
that snap like alligator teeth.

Now we're a coil, a circle, a group of people protesting the
Fu Manchu film, outdoors in rough terrain, a coil of shouting,
chanting people moving in a circle, sturdy, unending,
pulling us in, holding us up, covering the ground.

On the picket line the women's voices are the strongest.
One Chicana's voice rises, a tough wire in the wind,
leading the changes.

(1983)

Door to Door

All blabbing at once of course,
we raise our hands, the phone rings,
I grab the receiver to find
a hot iron aimed at my ear,
then chase after Pat explaining
we've got to fix the place in
that leaflet where the spelling is
backwards, but she's one block
ahead selling the *freedom*
socialist door to door I ring
the bell of where I used to live
a woman opens a sliver of my house,
says, "we don't want any," "but I
used to live here," I trail off
wondering if those fig trees
are still in the backyard,
the pale green ripe sweet figs. . .
the next person, mowing a lawn,
looks vague and familiar
in the same beard as 10 years back,
"it's Carl," I say, "Carl Mosk,"
but he doesn't remember me
the paint jobs we used to share,
Carl rattling on about Capital;
now he teaches economics at UC
and isn't a Marxist and I am.
even when I was little
I would have liked dialectics
because it puzzled me so much
that we are the same, and not,
waking up each morning new
in our bodies and skinned knees.
how do I know who Carl is?
because he's changed less.

it takes a long minute for the
glimmer of recognition to cross
his face, and then the glimmer of fear.
why the fear? my short hair, the
paper in my hand, this voice of
revolutionary feminism, which he
buys, then hands, hot potato,
to his wife. "I'll take it to my
art class," she says, "there's lots
of lesbians there, they'll be
interested." "sure, they will,"
I agree, wondering how she thinks
she knows, my short hair?
women's faces strong out from the page?
Carl smiles uneasy, starts the
motor, crops the lawn short
as I knock at the next door.

(1983)

Drawing the Line

1. Firing Line

Notice of Proposed Removal Action

Loyalty Board
Post Office Department, Washington D.C.

In the Matter of the Loyalty of Harriet M. Pierce
Seattle, Washington   Loyalty Case Number 6

Executive Order 9835, March 21, 1948
established a Federal Employees Loyalty Program
to see that disloyal civilian officers or employees
are not retained.

As the result of a recent investigation
made of you as an employee of the Post Office

information has been received
which indicates you have been
and that you are
affiliated or sympathetic with

an organization, association, movement, group
or combination of persons
designated as subversive

and on the basis of this evidence
grounds exist
for belief
that you are disloyal
to the Government of the United States

2. Holding the Line

We have lists
of those who stepped
across that line
to join us.
A piece of paper.
A simple list
of our party,
movement,
association,
group,
and combination of persons.
The names are the names
of those who stepped
across that line
to join us.
We stand in lines that stretch beyond
the law.
We march and are arrested.
We do not let the right wing
break our lines.
We say we have the right
to freedom of speech
to freedom of silence.
We say what we know
to be truth for the record.
We refuse to name names.
Subversive we shove back.
Loyal, we hold in trust
each name given.
It is that difficult
and that simple.

(1985)

Survivors

Survivors. Reading about the glow boys this morning.
The unemployed enticed with $60 to fix the core
of the nuclear plant. In space suits they jump
down into it. Acid rain, acid fog. "Just brush it off."
The screen I stare at, typesetting, low level,
the low lying words. Statistics for jumpers:
only one fatal cancer per 100. *Only!*

You look around to make sense of the forms,
bodies glowing with pain, campfires flickering
in the Oakland hills, where people are living in the rain,
no place else to go. The tv camera, hungry for news,
searches out the clammy tent where children lie bundled,
then leaves.

Every fact adds up but the word *depression* still
isn't officially used.

Survival is a repetitive process, days revolving
tasks completed or not, new ones streaming before you,
each day centered around food and sleep and wake
and talk. You follow this pattern of living set by
the dark and the light. Or break into pockets of
humming night, awake, catching up, getting ahead,
if only all the time could be used.

Surviving my mother's and grandmother's deaths this year,
sets me singular into the world. Finally not webbed
in their common life. Not directed or defined by
their concern or need or even love. No longer
a daughter. No longer younger.

The transitory myth of family. All we've ever had
to believe we belong.

Yet I belong. To the glow boys, to the people
camping in the hills, to young girls asking
for regard and strength, the food waiting to be
cooked for all. Yet I belong to those I touch
and work with. And to the dead also, and what
they have done. And whose beliefs and laughter
run through me and whose silence I turn to words.

My grandmother is that old woman in her patchwork
clothes, homeless, hat over thin grey hair,
pushing a cart of tin cans along Market Street.

(1981)

*Multi-talented
Karen Brodine.*

In Memory of Karen

O body swayed to music, O brightening glance,
How can we know the dancer from the dance?
                                           —W.B. Yeats

KAREN BRODINE was barely 40 years old when she died of cancer on October 18, 1987. Her death was a shock, a misery, an abrupt and unwarranted end to an exceptionally dynamic and productive life.

The horrible thing is that Karen's death was *unnecessary.* Cancer killed her because the medical profession was too profit-motivated, too sexist, to catch it in time, when they could and should have. And she was mad as hell at the medical automatons who prescribed the massive doses of poison known as chemotherapy when an ounce of prevention could have saved her.

Still, Karen was no martyr. She didn't waste a minute bemoaning her fate. She continued to the end to illuminate the aspirations, agonies, ironies, and triumphs of working people. She continued to share her vast artistic and political gifts with her comrades, co-workers, friends, and reading public, riveting audiences with her powerful words and her passionate and intensely earnest or wickedly witty presentation.

She left a rich and unforgettable legacy. Work, personal life, art, entertainment, organizing and ideas merged for her into one interrelated and total commitment to a future where everyone would live a full and integrated existence. She prescribed and brilliantly achieved "a *balance and a strong connection*

between dreaming, working, political action, loving. All ought
to be recognized and woven together into a tough, resistant
fabric."*

Hers was a cleanly congruent personality without a trace of
neurotic inner conflicts, despite the vast diversity of her interests
and variegated facets of her character. With a mind tough as
leather and a tongue to match, and a gentle sensitivity that
opened to the world, she synthesized, exemplified the best of
modern woman. She was something else—a paragon.

A multi-dimensional artist

Karen's original dream was to be a dancer.

She studied ballet and modern dance from the age of five
and majored in dance at the University of California at Berkeley,
graduating in 1972. She was a dance instructor for the
Richmond and Berkeley school districts and performed with the
Movable Feast Dance Group in the San Francisco Bay Area
until, in her 20s, a congenital knee problem ended her career.

Poetry then became her major artistic outlet.

And being Karen—the outgoing introvert—she felt
compelled to share her gift, to inspire others to tap their own
talents. She had first bloomed as a teacher in the mid-'60s.
Fresh out of highschool, she tutored reading and writing as a
volunteer for VISTA in Harlem, New York. Then, after receiving
an M.A. in Creative Writing from San Francisco State University
in 1974, she lovingly taught writing there, part-time, for six
years.

For students gripped by the inability to express themselves,
she labored to impart the understanding of imagery and how to
release it. In her poem "Fireweed" (included in this collection),
she informs us that images "live and breathe."

> . . .livewire sparks
> between opposites, a bridge that smokes between people.
> And that those most pushed down have the most to say
> in images, shouts, actions, all just under the smooth
> velour of the manufactured stories. Images leap out
> of contradiction, blasting the true story into breath.

* Karen Brodine, "Politics of Women Writing," *The Second Wave*, Vol. 5, no. 3
  (Summer/Fall 1979): 7.

Images, shouts, actions. Karen was an activist par excellence.

She co-founded the Women Writers Union in San Francisco in the early '70s. She was founding co-editor of the Kelsey Street Press and an editor at the Berkeley Poets Co-op. She was a proud and energetic member of the National Women Studies Association and the National Writers Union.

But how did she support herself? She turned to typesetting for her livelihood, a skill she loved for its integration of language, design and technology. A worker in the trade from 1975 to 1986, her intense and vivid experiences at work were central to her colorful poetry. All the craftsmanship, the mechanics and the nerve-endings of her profession come alive in her great poem, "Woman Sitting at the Machine, Thinking."

The art of politics

Karen was raised in a home environment of radical politics in rural Woodinville, Washington. She was especially proud of the intransigence of her grandmother, Harriet Pierce, a socialist postal worker who was identified as a subversive during the McCarthy period and was hounded by the FBI and forced to appear before the House Committee on Un-American Activities in 1955. She refused to testify and was blacklisted for her defiance, her union work and her strong, "premature" feminist beliefs.

Her mother, Mary, and father, Val, were also radicals, who supported themselves as music teachers. Their conflicts, ending in divorce, instilled Karen's iron-willed commitment to women's emancipation.

Karen moved to the Bay Area in the mid-'60s and weathered her own marriage and divorce, documented in her first book, *Slow Juggling*. She got involved in the feminist and lesbian/gay movements, became a socialist feminist and was soon a national leader of Radical Women and the Freedom Socialist Party, revolutionary feminist and multi-racial organizations. She was San Francisco organizer for Radical Women from 1979-81, and FSP organizer from 1981-83. From 1982 she served energetically on the FSP's National Committee.

Another major achievement was her coordination of the Merle Woo Defense Committee (1982-84). Her brilliant organizing skills, articulate advocacy talents, and fabled persistence were decisive in winning Woo's landmark suit against the University of California at Berkeley. Woo had charged discrimination on the basis of race, sex, sexual orientation, and political ideology, and was totally vindicated after long legal battles.

Karen returned to the Pacific Northwest in 1984 in order to edit, design and publish Gloria Martin's *Socialist Feminism: The First Decade, 1966-76*, a lively history of the early years of the Freedom Socialist Party.

Amid her publishing activity, Karen leapt into the political fray. The Seattle branch of the FSP was immersed in a legal battle known as the Freeway Hall Case, marked by the party's refusal to turn over membership lists and minutes of its meetings to the courts. The case began when a disgruntled male ex-FSP member, in a redbaiting frenzy, launched an incredible suit to recover a donation he made years earlier toward replacing the party's old headquarters at Freeway Hall, from which the party had been evicted.

Karen plunged into this fight for elemental civil liberties. She was struck by the parallel between the struggles of grandmother Harriet Pierce and the current FSP conflict. This catalyst engendered her poem "Drawing the Line" (published in this volume).

Far from seeking the rarefied isolation aspired to by many pompous writers, Karen invariably found daily political life to be a rich source of inspiration for vaulting poetry rooted in reality.

A wonderful life beautifully lived

Karen underwent surgery in 1986 for breast cancer and then had to endure a harrowing course of chemotherapy. But in spring 1987 she discovered that the cancer had metastisized. She was terminally ill. She fought heroically to overcome or stabilize her condition. She hated the idea of dying and was determined to live. She kept on writing, and she shared her poetry at public readings.

But when the pain and the struggle grew overwhelming, she knew the end was in sight, and she calmly, oh-so-efficiently, arranged her legal, artistic, financial, political and personal affairs, and bid her adieus. She hated to leave but she calmly called to say goodbye. Meanwhile, she had honed, planned, and directed this final collection of her work, entrusting her comrade Helen Gilbert with the awesome task of publishing it.

Until the day she died, in that memorable October of 1987, Karen never stopped being keenly concerned with current events, feminist issues, leftwing ideological debates, cultural developments, and the welfare of her comrades and family. She found solace in the companionship of loved ones, in the beauty of nature, in a Las Vegas gambling spree, in good cuisine (she relished Pacific Northwest seafood), and when she was confined to her bed, in the best of TV and Hollywood. She'd get so excited by good TV programs! She wanted to squeeze everything into her rapidly shortening life.

Throughout her valiant battle against the ravages of cancer, and through her final days, she transmitted an incredible persona. Dignity, courage, honesty, high awareness, and a fierce anger superceded by a practical acceptance of fate. She taught her friends and comrades well—about how to live and how to die, about the incredible human powers of resistance, strength, self-awareness and acceptance up to the finish line.

Oh, hell. She shouldn't have been taken from us. She was so strong, so vital, so needed, so loved and respected. So much fun to be around.

She was a radical poet and a poetic radical. . .a revolutionary artist and an artistic revolutionary. . .a feminist thinker and a thinking woman. . .an ultimate person for all seasons and all stages of the game. Her loss was incalculable, inconsolable. But her heritage is eternal and universal. In her the dancer and the dance coalesced; she was all of a piece, all together.

Janet Sutherland
Seattle, Washington
January 1988

Compendium of Karen Brodine's Writings

Books

Slow Juggling. Berkeley: Berkeley Poets Cooperative, 1975.

Workweek. Berkeley: Kelsey St. Press, 1977.

Illegal Assembly. Brooklyn, New York: Hanging Loose Press, 1980.

Criticism

"Politics of Women Writing." *The Second Wave*, Vol. 5, no. 3 (Summer/Fall 1979): 6-13.

Essays

"Ancient Matriarchy and Modern Feminism." *Radical Women Internal Discussion Bulletin*, Vol. 11, no. 2 (December 1981): 1-13.

"Giving Criticism Arms." *FSP Pre-Convention Bulletin*, No. 3 (April 26, 1982): 7-12.

Introduction to *Socialist Feminism: The First Decade, 1966-1976*, by Gloria Martin. Seattle: Freedom Socialist Publications, 1986.

Articles

"Can Charlie Chan." *Freedom Socialist*, Vol. 6, no. 3 (Summer/Fall 1980): 10.

"Women and Porno." *Freedom Socialist*, Vol. 6, no. 3 (Summer/Fall 1980): 15.

"Merle Woo Fights for the Right to Teach." *Freedom Socialist*, Vol. 8, no. 1 (Fall 1982): 5, 24.

"Judge Orders: Rehire Merle Woo!" *Freedom Socialist*, Vol. 8, no. 2 (Spring 1983): 6.

"Merle Woo's Labor/Civil Rights Case: From Campus to Courtroom." *Freedom Socialist*, Vol. 8, no. 3 (Summer 1983): 1.

"Merle Woo. . .Never a Victory so Sweet!" *Freedom Socialist*, Vol. 9, no. 1 (Autumn 1984): 1.

Interviews

"A Conversation with Nellie Wong and Merle Woo, Poet-Radicals." *Freedom Socialist*, Vol. 7, no. 1 (Spring 1981): 7.

Credits

*Cover by Eve Anthony • Book design and production by Helen Gilbert •
Editorial/technical assistance by Clara Fraser, Mike Warner,
Tamara Turner, Raya Fidel and Gaby Garza*

Typeset in Korinna and Benguiat by Imageset, Mercer Island, Washington

Red Letter Press & Freedom Socialist Publications

The Indian-Sandinista War in Nicaragua
by Yolanda Alaniz

TOWARDS the '90s:
Approaching the Final Conflict
by Guerry Hoddersen and Clara Fraser

Gay Resistance:
The Hidden History
by Sam Deaderick and Tamara Turner

Socialist Feminism the first decade 1966-76
gloria martin
introduction by karen brodine

A Victory for Socialist Feminism

BARRON'S
Black Monday

AIDS Hysteria
A Marxist Analysis
by Stephen Durham & Susan Williams, MD

Revolutionary Integration
Yesterday and Today
Tom Boot

the freedom socialist
Now is the time for a
LABOR PARTY

The Chicano Struggle:
a racial or a national movement?
— Yolanda Alaniz and Megan Cornish

THE WAR ON THE DISABLED:
Adding Insult to Injury
by Heidi Durham

Write for a complete list of titles to Red Letter Press,
5018 Rainier Ave. South, Seattle, WA 98118 • 206-722-2453